MW00900541

Copyright Information

ISBN 9781704318585

Independently Published

First Edition: November 2019

www.thatdamnlawyer.com

That Damn Lawyer Presents:
The Entity Formation Handbook

By:
Brian H. Hanning
www.thatdamnlawyer.com

Welcome Reader

Reader,

I would love to tell you I started my law firm for some altruistic reason, to save the world. Or, because I grew up knowing I would own my own business one day and after going through law school immediately decided to hang a shingle.

No, the truth is both stranger and simpler. I had an internship right out of law school and when that ended, I found a position as the only associate in a previously one person shop. When I stepped away from the firm, I had a couple of clients wanting to follow me and a new client asking about a project.

Of course, without knowing what I was doing, I agreed. Soon, I had my company formed, with a bank account and everything, and was out trying to drum up additional business. That was June.

It wasn't until December that I took the time to slow down and really delve into a business plan.

Running a business is complicated and it can be incredibly rewarding. You get to be the boss, the salesman, the person doing the actual work of the business, and everything in between. I, in all honesty, love it. I can also see how all this legal stuff can be daunting.

That is why I wrote this Handbook, and others, to help people in similar situations answer some of those legal questions. Law ends up being behind the scenes in so many ways in our lives. Whether we are out making a documentary or installing windows, driving packages or creating marketing.

Each topic I cover is something relevant to one kind of business or another, be it a hobby turned side gig such as a photo challenge or a passion project turned day job or any other situation where you become your own boss.

Which may raise the question of why listen to me?

The answer being, this is what I do in my day job. I help small businesses understand law. I get to help people understand why some document or concept is needed. Every day at my law firm, I help businesses in one way or another.

I know many people start their business on the smallest of budgets. Searching for answers or guidance to fit your business can be daunting. I highly suggest getting in contract with your local resources, such as: the Small Business Development Centers, business and non-profit resource librarians, or pro bono centers such as the Attorneys for the Arts programs. It is in making connections and meeting the right resources which can help you be successful in all of your goals.

And so, Reader, welcome to this Handbook.

I will say that once you read this and if it is something that resonates with you, please keep it close to hand. Sometimes, being able to double check can help keep things clear for you.

Best of luck with your endeavors!

Brian H. Hanning

www.thatdamnlawyer.com

Table of Contents

Introduction

Starting a business is an exciting and challenging process. There is a joy and freedom in being able to choose your path on your own terms. The satisfaction of building something from scratch is a big bonus.

Your business starts as an idea, a dream, a passion project. Your business has the opportunity to grow from inspiration into an income producing company. Part of the way to encourage growth is to have a structure: the legal entity.

In addition, growth comes from operations, and a new business owner may find themselves needing to be the expert in a number of different fields. That can include needing expertise in:

Accounting

Operations and Planning

Marketing and Social Media Marketing

Technical know-how

- Sales

- Customer Service

And many more as the business starts to grow.

These demands are why you should consider connecting with external experts to learn what you need to create your business and allow your business to thrive under your leadership.

Building a team of trusted resource providers in your local community can help you get out of the minutia of operating the business and instead let you focus on core competencies with the product(s) or service(s) you want to deliver.

Also, it can be a lot of fun to connect with other business owners - sharing interests, challenges, and skills.

If you have your inspiration and are looking to start a business, this Handbook is for you. We will discuss how to set up the legal entity to allow you to build your dream business.

Section A: Disclosures

As a lawyer, I support and educate people about legal issues and concerns for their business, including how decisions can affect their rights and quality of life. The majority of this Handbook is attuned providing expert advice to help you start your business, and to keep your sanity as much as possible throughout.

This Handbook covers the topic of entity formation and some issues likely to arise in the process. These resources and comments are provided for guidance and general assistance. Very little law is quoted and any opinions as to the law are generalizations. This Handbook is based on United States law, and the specifics around entity formation are determined per State Law.

No attorney client relationship is formed by the basis of referring to this book. If legal assistance is needed, it is best for you to find local attorney with expertise and experience in your geographical area.

Section B: Planning for Success

Before getting all into the legal concerns, I want to touch on business plans. A business plan is a roadmap describing the focus and goals of the business. This could include:

- Mission and vision statements

- Plan of action

- Clarity related to deliverables - product(s) or service(s)

- Target markets and marketing strategies

- Financial statements and documents

And other important details.

A business plan can be essential for any business owners and especially helpful for first time entrepreneurs. The business plan can help in distinguishing entities and the goals of different businesses for serial entrepreneurs. When you are looking for funding from outside investors, or even banks, such a plan may be required.

4

Article 1: What is an Entity and Why Form One

Section A: What is an Entity?

At the simplest level, an entity is a legal construct acting as an independent person. Alternatively, an entity is a piece of paper treated as a person. Another definition is a collection of statutory requirements, filings, and internal description documents. This definition is less usable on a practical level in terms of daily operations, but it is helpful from a legal perspective.

In the context of an entity, a "person" does not mean a living breathing human - it means a construct recognized by law. This recognition includes certain rights and abilities. Both the rights and abilities necessary to operate as a business, along with a vigorous debate as to such additional rights and abilities an entity can utilize. For the purpose of this Handbook, we will stick to what is generally accepted.

In defining what an entity is, many times there is a reference to how the entity is structured, how it acts, and perhaps most importantly, how it is taxed. In other words, the type of entity "defines" how the business is treated, taxed, and operates.

These definitions are offered to help give you an idea of what we are discussing. As we move forward in this Handbook, we will discuss some details about the differences between entities and various rules associated with each entity. As a starting point, the definition should be based on the core features of almost any entity. **Specifically, as stated, an entity is a (1) a legal construct that (2) acts as (3) an independent person.**

Subsection 1: A Legal Construct

Every entity is a "Legal Construct." Which means approximately nothing, in the practical world. Instead, let's step back a moment to refresh ourselves on some basic civics.

Legislators at the statehouse, your local congress, passes laws. Those laws cover many, many subjects - traffic, marriage, divorce, and most pertinent to this discussion, business. Some of the most and least controversial of these are the laws related to how an entity is identified and how it operates. In essence, an entity is a construct defined by and constrained by the statutes describing it.

These laws do not cover everything, and sometimes, the laws do not adequately address your most important concerns. The laws create the bare necessities of any and every entity recognized in a State.

mentioned an entity can be talked about as a "Person," this is where the analogy breaks. A human being, a person, has independent action in and of themselves. An entity does not. Instead, the entity is given form through statutes and given mobility through human action.

For example, do you need to manufacture something? The laws outlining the entity allows for employees that act as the entities hands". Need to decide to purchase office A or office B? The laws outlining the entity provides for one or more owners to make the decision and others like it. Need to sue someone? The law allows for that as well.

A key thing to remember is most laws related to entity formation do not have significant limitations on "action." Laws do exist to regulate action, but we are not going to address them in this Handbook. However, the laws describing the entity deal with the most generic description of the entity possible - i.e. a corporation has a board of directors and officers with specific duties. Most everything else is left to the entity to determine, in compliance with all relevant law.

Subsection 2: The Acts of the Entity

An entity has the ability to act. This is a strange statement to make when referring to what is essentially a piece of paper complying with statutes read pretty much only by attorney's. However, independent action is what makes the entity "viable" or a "business".

An entity can do a lot of things, but it acts through humans or "people". Now remember, the actions of those people taken on behalf of the entity are <u>attributed</u> to the entity itself.

Take for example recalled products. They are not considered the fault of the individual(s) who designed the product, the fault of the individual(s) who manufactured the product, or even the fault of the individual(s) who sold the product. It is the fault of the entity causing the product to be designed, manufactured, and sold (if one entity or the manufacturing entity depending on the circumstance).

In other words, the entity acted to design, manufacture, or (and) sell the product, and thus, is the "person" ultimately responsible.

Entities are empowered to act in a variety and almost limitless ways, including but not limited to:

Selling ownership in the entity

Buying another entity

Selling services or products, or both

- Entering into contracts

- Hiring employees and independent contractors

- Suing and be sued

- Renting office space

And much more. The specific language tends to be similar to: **an entity is empowered to take any actions necessary pursue any lawful business**.

In other words, if a business venture is not explicitly prohibited by law - such as human trafficking or slavery, among others - an entity can act in any manner legally permitted in pursuing that venture.

Subsection 3: Entity as an Independent Person

This is perhaps one of the most important things. You, the owner, are not the entity. The entity is not you. Yes, in certain circumstances this "corporate veil" of liability protection can be collapsed. However, the baseline rule and generally accepted status - until proven otherwise - is the entity is a separate, independent person.

This means the liability for acts of the entity remains with the entity. It is generally not the liability of you or any person who performed or authorized the acts creating liability. This is a good rule of thumb to remember as a sole business owner. **The entity is not you and you are not the entity.**

For your reference, this separation is called the "corporate veil" in legal parlance. Proving there is no separation is referred to as "piercing the corporate veil," meaning the law sees right through the entity, the veil, to you, personally.

An important and practical note on maintaining the separate status of the entity: Please keep separate bank accounts and separate tax identification outside of your personal accounts and tax identification number. Separate and independent is the general rule, failing to take appropriate steps can lose this protection.

It is better to take more protections than you think you need, because you don't want to find out the protection is gone at the worst possible time - like in the middle of a lawsuit for example, which is when the corporate veil might be pierced.

Section B: Why use an Entity?

The "why" is answered primarily by reference to the separation discussion shared in the prior section. Separation of liability is a major feature and key benefit for business owners.

Take the example of manufacture and recall. A product tends not to be recalled unless there is significant harm to people associated with the product - disease, disability, death. However, the party at fault for causing such harm is the entity.

Not the owners, not the employees. The entity.

This reasoning may not seem that strong for an individual looking at starting a service business when working for yourself. However, the risks remain the same, if in different scope. A client can still be frustrated and attempt to sue you and the entity over the service offered. Or, a sole owner entity can still want to purchase a building and have the liability of the building - taxes, slip and falls claims, and the rest - associated with an entity instead of an owner.

In addition, any personal challenges you may have as an individual are not connected to the business. As a separate entity, the business remains safe and intact, even if you have personal challenges or are at fault in a car accident, as an example.

Now you have a good idea of what an entity is and why using an entity is best practice and highly recommended, the next question is: what kind of entity?

Article 2: Choice of Entity

As mentioned, an entity is defined by State law. By way of example, here are some of the types of entities you can create:

- Partnerships

- Corporations

- Limited Liability Companies

- Nonprofit corporations

- Cooperatives

- Partnerships

And many more.

This means there are two questions that should be answered to chose the type of entity.

- What types of entities exist in your State?

- What are your goals as the owner(s) of the entity?

Section A: Types of Entity

As entities are determined by the authorizations in statute, each State

has different entities permissible to be formed in the State. The

challenge is, entities may exist in some States but not others. In

addition, there are developments in how business is thought of and as

a result new types of entities are being created. For instance, there are

some entities proposed by think tanks looking at promoting some

particular types of actions over others.

As such, this Handbook will cover three entities.

The three Entities discussed in this Handbook are Corporations,

Limited Liability Companies, and Public Benefit Corporations. This is

not to discount or disregard other entities, I chose these three based

upon general needs and the developmental trend already mentioned

These are some of the most common and important entities. **To get**

specific, detailed information to determine the best Entity for you

it is best practice to find a local attorney who focuses on the

formation of Entities and can walk you through your options based upon your State.

First and foremost, it's important to choose an entity type to begin operating the business, to be granted the rights and abilities needed to operate officially. However, there is an option called conversion. It's a legal process of taking an existing entity and changing the underlying legal structure into a different type of entity, if at any point the structure needs to change to support the business more effectively. Other registrations, including tax numbers, remain valid.

If at any point you need to go through the conversion process, an accountant can help you understand the tax consequences and a lawyer can help you with the specific steps.

One last note on the entity of partnerships. A partnership is a sole proprietorship with more than one person. A sole proprietorship is an individual holding themselves out as doing business.

It is generally not advisable to operate as a sole proprietorship or partnership. These are "original" entities with one flaw that cannot be overcome. There is no separation between you and the partnership. This means you have no liability protection on a personal level. This lack of protection sidesteps the point of creating an entity in the first place.

Subsection 1: Corporation

The Corporation is an old type of entity. The first for profit corporation that sold stock was the East India Trading Company in the 1600's, and a decent amount of modern law relating to Corporations is derived from laws first written prior to the founding of the United States. Since there, there have been significant changes in how such statutes are understood and written.

A corporation is an entity with the well-known structure of Shareholders, a Board of Directors and has statutorily required officers. Ownership is defined through stock (or "shares") of the Corporation.

Decision making is generally split between Shareholders, the Board of Directors, and Officers. Each group has specific roles and responsibilities.

Shareholders primarily elect individuals to the Board and decide on high level strategic issues presented by the Board. These strategic issues can be anything from determinations related to approvals for mergers to support for or against amendments to governing documents.

The **Board of Directors** approves or rejects appointments of individuals as Officers, guides the overall direction of the Corporation, and provides guidance by voting to concerns presented by the Officers.

Officers are the hands that effectuate the intent of the Shareholders and Board through the lens of the purpose and capabilities of the Corporation. Officers can include:

- President

- Secretary

- Treasurer

- Vice President

- Vice Secretary

- Vice Treasurer

And others as needed by the Corporation.

Those roles labeled with a "Vice" may not be required, but are used to expand the effectiveness of the Officers. I will touch on specific roles more as we get into details about Bylaws, for now just know the Officers run the daily business of the Corporation.

Of course, other roles may be practical for your business, but the roles

mentioned above are statutorily required, reflecting the needs of the

entity and not necessarily the needs of your business.

Sub-Subsection I: Shareholders and Stock

Shareholders have been mentioned a couple of times. A shareholder

is an individual who holds stock or shares. Stock and shares are

almost, but not quite, interchangeable terms and I will use stock for

the rest of this Handbook.

Stock is the ownership interest for a Corporation. In other words, each

shareholder is an owner of the Corporation. Technically, the Board

and the Officers report to and act on behalf of the Shareholders.

There can be overlap among Shareholders, Board Members, and

Officers. However, just because a person is a Shareholder, they are not

guaranteed any other position - and vice versa.

The type of stock held defines the rights and duties given to the Shareholder. This can be in the form of voting rights, distribution rights, liquidation preferences, among others.

Upon formation, you determine a set number of stock to exist. This stock can be increased, in a process determined by each State and by the Corporation in the Bylaws.

The nice thing about stock is that it exists. In other words, if you form your Corporation with 1000 stocks, 1000 stocks exist.

You can issue some or all of the stock. Meaning, you can have stock in reserve for founders, for employees, or for investment. This has the effect of having authorized (your total amount of stock) and issued stock. It also means vesting - or earning ownership over time - is possible and fairly straight forward to implement.

Generally, stock is split between Preferred Stock and Common Stock, with the difference being around how those rights are defined. There no limit to the types of shares, but generally, more complicated share structures are reserved for larger companies that have a support staff to monitor and effectuate the distinctions.

Sub-Subsection II: Why choose a Corporation?

Now, with this fairly rigid structure and overall demands of the Corporation, the question would be - why choose it as the entity for your business? The answer is tied, in part, to the familiarity of the entity. In my opinion, a Corporation is a good fit for two groups of people:

1. Entities with an expectation of a large group of owners. As shareholders have limited ability to impact the daily operation of the Corporation, this allows groups with tens, hundreds, or more owners to be effective on a day to day basis as the Officers make operational decisions.

.   Corporations are preferred forms for entities seeking investment capital. While there are venture or other sources of capital that will work with different entity types, due to the way ownership is attached to stock, it makes investment more attractive to third

parties. Shares can also be modified by the Board as needed.

Investment dilutes current ownership, but dilution is different than

redistributing current ownership interests.

Overall, the combined positives and negatives of Corporations

balance out, making a definite place for them in the current economic

climate and in the future.

Subsection 2: Limited Liability Company

A Limited Liability Company, or LLC, is a fairly new entity type in legal

terms. LLC's as a concept were introduced in 1977 in Wyoming,

spreading through the 1990s to become an entity choice in all 50

States.

The core conceit of the LLC is to combine the entity flexibility of a

partnership with the liability protection of a Corporation. The practica

reality is an LLC is very attractive for a close ownership group, allowin

for a decent amount of flexibility of structure, and few limitations.

From a legal perspective, what this means is an LLC is a modification

of the partnership, with a number of important concepts being

derived from partnership law.

Sub-Subsection I: A Tangent to key partnership Law

am going to cover a couple of legal concepts brought to the LLC

rom partnerships. These concepts are the operating principles of an

LC. Unless they have been modified, which we will discuss when we

each the operating agreement.

he first concept is related to ownership of a partnership. In

artnerships, there are no shares, instead each partner gets an

interest." That interest can include some detail, but a major element

the percent of the partnership each owner receives. Keep in mind all

e ownership interest is held with none "leftover". A partnership is

00% owned at any given time.

s an example, four people start a partnership. They decide to keep it

mple and give each partner an equal interest, included is an equal percent of ownership. This means each partner owns 25% of the partnership, for a total of 100% ownership cumulative among the partners.

A different example is there are three people - Jane, Karen, and John - starting a partnership. Instead of having equal shares, the three decide to split it up according to expected involvement. Thus, Karen gets 45% ownership, Jane has 40%, and John rounds it out with 15%. Again, 100% of the partnership is owned.

Look back at stock under Corporations, it just exists. Meaning more can be created or set aside, "leftover" if you will. The same concept just doesn't exist in partnership based ownership.

Shifting slightly, each partner is an "agent"of the partnership, meaning each partner can legally bind the partnership acting independently. This can be helpful, allowing each partner to go out and do business on behalf of the partnership. On the other hand, any partner acting independently can do what they think is best.

What happens then when two partners go out independently and each sign different leases on behalf of the partnership? The answer is the partnership is legally obligated to follow both leases.

Partnerships are governed by a contract called a partnership agreement modifying essentially any of the statutory rules of partnerships. In an LLC, this is mirrored in the operating agreement, which we will delve into later in this Handbook.

An LLC is not a partnership. Meaning that while the concepts are the same, the naming conventions and specific aspects, such as liability protection for the owners, are different.

Where there are partners in a partnership, the LLC has one or more members. A partner holds an interest, a member holds a "Unit" of membership, equal to all other existing Units unless otherwise stated. As mentioned, a Unit is a different name for an interest. They have the same characteristics and functions. As such, an LLC, like a partnership, is at all times 100% owned. This can make certain things like vesting more challenging.

As in partnerships, each Member is an agent of the LLC, with all the benefits and challenges already mentioned.

Sub-Subsection II: What did the Corporation add?

In the introduction to LLCs, I said the LLC combines "the entity flexibility of a partnership with the liability protection of a Corporation." That means an LLC is not just a differently worded partnership, concepts from the Corporation had to be included.

The inclusion from the Corporation is the reason why LLCs are preferred over partnerships by attorneys. Specifically, the LLC includes the corporate veil from the Corporation. You as a Member are protected and you are not held individually liable for any wrong doing of the LLC.

The corporate veil is the most important addition, but not the only one. Specifically, there is the idea of Managers.

Now, the rules vary from State to State, but the basic concept is the Members are generally the individual(s) who are operating the Entity, the agents of the LLC. Electing at formation into a Manager- Managed scheme means Members become like Shareholders.

With a Manager, Members do not need to participate in the daily operations. One or more Managers act as all the Officers of the Corporation wrapped into one title.

Sub-Subsection III: Why Choose an LLC?

In a lot of formation discussions, the decision process is framed as:

You are an LLC unless you really need to be a different entity.

A big reason for this is the simplification of structure. Where a Corporation has one or more classification of shareholders, a Board of Directors, Officers, and then employees, the LLC is streamlined. At the simplest, an LLC is a Member and employees. Even at the most complicated, there are Members, Managers, and employees.

This means decision making operations and taking action can be fairly efficient.

A few words of warning when considering an LLC. LLCs are uniquely qualified for what entrepreneurs terms "lifestyle" businesses. The idea being the business can support the lifestyle of the owner and may be passed down through generations of the family. They are not designed to easily facilitate outside investment.

Why? At any one time 100% of the LLC is owned. If an investor wants to invest into the LLC, the investor has to work through the Members. The investor must purchase part or all of the Membership Unit of one or more Members. This can make it emotionally difficult and logistically challenging to accomplish.

For entrepreneurs, this 100% ownership has some other trickle down effects, most notably in vesting. In a number of startups, there is the idea of paying key employees in vesting ownership. There are work arounds for LLCs, but it is not true vesting and may not be the best choice for your entity.

If you are looking at an LLC and significant investment or vesting, a different entity may be better. If you are just one person building your dream job, an LLC can be the best entity to chose.

Subsection C: Public Benefit Corporation

As might be inferred from the name, the Public Benefit Corporation, or PBC, is a variant of the Corporation. Since enacted as a statute in Maryland in 2010, the PBC has spread but is not yet fully be adopted by all Fifty States. So, why are we talking about the PBC?

In the academic and litigation communities of businesses and law, a prevalent theory about Corporations exists. Specifically, the corporation must act to maximize shareholder revenue. Regardless of the truth of the theory, court decisions and law have, at times, used the theory.

There are those who look at this specific theory of Corporations and demand more. The PBC provides a legal mandate to consider and take actions that support a public benefit - in essence expanding the purview of the Corporation from pure profit motive to social considerations.

The PBC generally requires three things:

1. One or more Public Benefit Director(s) on the Board

2. One or more Public Benefit Officer(s)

3. and an annual report accessible to the public about the steps taken for the Public Benefit.

Beyond that, a PBC is a Corporation, with all that entails and as we have previously discussed.

Keeping that in mind, I want to discuss the movement towards social responsible legal entities. In the mid-1990s the triple bottom line movement started. The Triple Bottom line, crafted by John Elkington states a business should focus on profits, planet, and people. This started picking up attention and soon was a common business theory, even if not widely used in practice.

In 2007, a non-profit called B-Lab started issuing B-Corp Certifications to other organizations, recognizing them for specific actions. The certifications were awarded on the principle of "products, practices, and profits, businesses should aspire to do no harm and benefit all" while being "responsible for each other and future generations." See https://bcorporation.net/about-b-corps.

It was B-Lab who introduced the model statute for the PBC and push for it's adoption.

This entity is a step towards statutory and legal requirements to help businesses consider consequences of their actions beyond profit margins. Other entities may be created with more expansive social demands than the PBC. For now, the PBC represents an entity on the leading edge of legal and business theory on best practices.

Sub-Subsection I: Why use a PBC?

All of this may seem like academic so and so. The truth is, the PBC can be the right entity for you. Unlike an LLC, the PBC has the ownership structure of stocks just like a Corporation - making investment easier.

In addition, many entrepreneurs are trying to change the world, in their own way. Sometimes, it is small and local, other times they see a major problem in the world and are trying to fix it. Depending on your goals and desires, having an entity with a partial focus on social needs can be just right.

Just keep in mind, the law around PBCs are new and evolving. Currently, there is a gap between what is affirmatively stated and what a court may interpret the statutes to mean. This entity is similar to a lot of entrepreneurs: there is risk, but there is also reward.

Section B: Identify Goals

Now, armed with some basic information on entities, it is time to get to choosing the right entity for you.

Some may say choice of entity is mostly a legal and accounting function. My opinion is choice of entity should be based on your goals, personally and for the business. The best thing to do is to talk through the choice with a trusted confidant to connect with the type of entity with the best fit and to gain a clear understanding of the strengths and weaknesses of the structure.

As a baseline for the discussion, let's start with a question: What is the goal of the business?

Is the goal to:

- Bring a community together to make a specific thing less expensive or better? Perhaps a cooperative makes the most sense.
- Make a profit sufficient to provide a certain lifestyle for the owners and employees? Perhaps an LLC is the entity to chose.

  Earn a profit while making the community better through a form of stewardship? Then the PBC should be investigated, or the Low -Profit Limited Liability Corporation, if available in your State.

- Gather massive amounts of venture capital or other investment needed to develop a product that will alter human development on the scale of smart phones? A Corporation is a strong candidate.

Now, just because an entity is named here as an example doesn't mean it is the best choice. More importantly it may not be the right choice for you.

It depends on:

- Your product or service

- What entities available in your State

- The ownership group itself.

A perfect example could be a lifestyle business, with ownership spread among four friends. One friend is the money and the others are going to participate by running daily operations. An LLC may make sense to reach the end goal, but other factors such as the number of owners could shift the entity of choice it towards a

Corporation. Or perhaps, in this situation the group is starting a

community farm and a Cooperative is ideal for the stated goal.

The more an ownership group can identify the goals and motivations

of the business, the better a fit the entity is likely to be.

And remember, because an entity has been chosen doesn't mean you

can't convert entities to be a different entity type to better reach

evolving goals and ownership. There will be a cost and the process is

governed by the State, but there is always a choice. Just confirm with

lawyer, an accountant, and co-owners if you are ready to make a

change, and then connect with the state government for the

appropriate paperwork.

Article 3: Registrations: Secretary of State, EIN, Licenses

Once a decision has been made about what entity type, it's time to tell the appropriate governmental agencies. This Article covers three big registrations and filings every business should have, or at the very least look into obtaining.

I am going to broadly cover registering with the Secretary of State, obtaining an Employer Identification Number, and applying for any other licenses necessary.

Section A: The Secretary of State

Generally speaking the Secretary of State has a couple of roles, from running elections to registering businesses. It is the business side of things which we will discuss here.

Each Secretary of State is empowered by their State to collect and publish certain public records related to businesses. These filings can be any number of things, and may be titled something different in each state. For example, businesses can file with their Secretary of State a "trade name" or a "doing business as" name - the difference being what the State calls the filing.

There are two main types of filing in relation to the formation of a business. Specifically the registration document of the business - such as the Articles of Incorporation or the Articles of Organization. Articles of Incorporation tend to apply to any Corporation based entity, such as:

- Non-profits

- Public benefit corporations, and

- Corporations.

Articles of Organization tend to apply to:

- Limited Liability Company's

- Cooperatives - generally, and

- Such other entities that are similar to LLCs.

Because each State has different laws, there may be particular areas of information a State may request unique to that State.

Standard requests include:

- Business Name with appropriate naming convention

- Street and mailing addresses of the business

- Entity specifics - classes of shares, manager or member managed

- Name and address of the registered Agent, and

- Signature of an individual authorized to make the filing.

Two questions generally arise from these requirements:

1. What is a registered agent?

2. Who should be in that position?

A registered agent is the person or entity designated by a business to accept certain paperwork. The registered agent must be physically present in the State where the entity is registered. Typically this includes announcements about needing to file annual reports and to receive service of a lawsuit.

As to who should be the registered agent? It depends on your State and your needs. While States can be permissive, allowing the entity itself to act as the registered agent, most of the time a registered agent is a third party. Meaning you as the owner or someone you hire. If you are going to hire, there are professional registered agent services and some accountants or attorneys also provide registered agent services.

Most importantly make sure whoever is appointed is comfortable with the role. You, or whom ever is hired, should be prepared for and understand what being the registered agent for the business means. Registrations with the Secretary of State are official documents. As such, knowingly filing without authorization or knowingly filing a false statement is illegal. Always make sure everything is true and accurate before filing. If the business owner is not the one filing it, ensure the filer has explicit authorization and all relevant information to complete the filing accurately.

Keep in mind States adopt technology at different rates. Some States allow for all Secretary of State filings to be done online. Others require filings to be by United States Postal Service or in person. Some offices allow both filing methods, depending on circumstances.

Section B: EIN and other Tax Registrations

Tax related regulations and laws are complicated. It is best practice talk to an accountant before taking any action with regard to the IRS.

The Employer Identification Number, the EIN, is the number given to n entity by the Internal Revenue Service. The number is used to track nd identify the tax information related to the entity.

Getting an EIN is not too difficult. Go to https://www.irs.gov/ usinesses/small-businesses-self-employed/apply-for-an-employer-entification-number-ein-online. There is a web app that guides a gistering individual through the process.

Depending on the entity there are a number of decision points.

However, most decisions are tied to an LLC. The IRS broadly

recognizes three types of businesses:

- Sole ownerships

- Partnerships, and

- Corporations.

LLCs get to elect out of partnership taxation and into corporate

taxation, if desired. If you are the only owner of an LLC, the IRS may

tax the entity on your Social Security or other personal tax

identification number.

This choice can have significant tax consequences, it is best to discuss

with your accountant before obtaining the number.

While this is the only federal tax registration required at formation,

there may be some other choices. For example, you may want to elect

into Subsection S taxation, commonly referred to as an S-Corporation.

Or it may be important to file a Form 1023 to register as a tax exempt entity under Section 501C. Either way, these are tax elections that layer over the entity and change it's taxation.

Again, while an attorney can assist, it is best practice to speak with an accountant about such issues.

Finally, there may be tax registrations in the local State, County, or Municipality - all of which very depending on your location. At the State and Local levels, most tax registrations are sales tax licenses. Some municipalities use sales tax licenses as a general business license with all businesses required to obtain a sales tax license, regardless of if the business would remit sales taxes. It is best to consult with an accountant or attorney familiar with your State and municipality to get the best course of action.

Section C: Licenses

There are a number of different types of licenses, and which ones exist and are necessary depend on your State and Municipality. These can include anything from a business license to approval to act as a regulated business. We are going to focus on a couple types of licenses you may need.

Common licenses apply to specifically governed and monitored businesses. These licenses to apply to "sin" businesses and "licensed" professions.

Those sin businesses include alcohol ("liquor laws" typically) and marijuana licenses. These can apply to any business in the supply chain where the end result is a consumer purchasing alcohol or marijuana.

Licensed professions are broader, and most likely listed under a Department of Regulated Activities. These licenses can include everything from barbers to massage therapists, and from architects to mortuaries. Each State regulates different professions (with overlap, of course) and regulates those professions as determined by the State in order to protect consumers from a variety of concerns.

Generally, applications can be done by a lay person, but consulting with an expert may be helpful to ensure you are covering everything required and obtaining the correct licenses.

Article 4: Governing Documents

When starting a business, there is a bit more legal work than is routinely thought. While registering with appropriate governmental agencies is important, think back to the reason for entities in the first place. Specifically, the limitation of liability by virtue of the separation between owner and business.

One way to ensure the separation is to look at and use the formalities given by the statutes. This includes approving and following a governing document.

This Article is going to cover bylaws and operating agreements. These documents are the "governing" documents, the "constituent" documents, or the "background" documents. These documents are designed to outline how a business operates along with roles and responsibilities.

Section A: Bylaws

Bylaws govern Corporations and similar entities. There are some "formulaic" provisions and a number of sections required for any business.

In some ways, bylaws don't feel as connected to the daily operation o the business. To a degree this is true, but it can also mean that the "standard" and "formulaic" bylaws need modification focusing on meaning and usefulness.

Bylaws expand upon the Articles of Incorporation, explaining the key statements around ownership while also providing the highest levels of organizational structure.

For example, the Articles of Incorporation list how many classes of stock exist and some modicum of description for those stocks. The Bylaws delve into the differentiating aspects of the different types of shares to a greater degree. This may include:

- Voting rights

- Liquidation rights

- Dividend rights

- Inspection of records rights

- Limitations on sales of stock

And more.

Each right can be treated individually (Such as Class A and Class B being equal except for Liquidation rights) or all the rights can be created collectively (Such as Class A being elevated in all categories when compared to Class B) depending on the needs of the business or the stock. This is an opportunity to create fairly traditional stocks, or to get a little inventive with mixing and matching rights - it's up to you based on the needs of your business at inception or as later determined.

Bylaws also need some very specific sections, such as sections on management including describing Directors and Officers.

For Directors, the Bylaws may identify the number of Directors on the Board and how the Shareholder votes for a Director. This is another area where voting can be creative - in giving certain stocks more votes, allowing for a person with multiple stocks to vote them all on the same Director, or in a scheme which best fits your business. Directors are empowered to vote on strategic items and have the power to appoint the President and other Officers. Remember, the Officers have specific roles as provided by statute and are the people who operate the business at the highest level.

Roughly, the President controls operations and is the individual making day to day decisions. The Secretary keeps the books in regard to shareholders, who is a current owner and what notices the owners are due. The Treasurer is the one who signs the checks and determines financial considerations. The Bylaws generally explain how Officers are appointed, what their specific roles are, and similar concerns.

Bylaws also cover provisions related to meetings, including:

- How often are regular meetings held? Once a year or more frequently?

- What about special meetings for if an issue arises in between regular meetings?

- How are the Shareholders and Directors notified about such meetings?

- Can the Directors attend by video conferencing or other virtual means?

Bylaws are more expansive, including provisions about amending the bylaws and conflict of interest statements - among others. These provisions are focused on the needs of the business in particular or can seem overly simplistic, such as provisions on corporate purpose and office location.

Even if Bylaws are found as templates or purchased from a service, it can be a good idea to have them reviewed by a professional to confirm viability and usability based upon your State's laws.

Section B: Operating Agreement

For entities not based on Corporation governing principles, there still needs to be some understanding of who is making decisions and how those decisions are made. While Corporation based governance is through Bylaws, most other types of entities use a form of contract instead. For an LLC, the contract is called an Operating Agreement, between all Members of the LLC.

Because the Operating Agreement has the same purpose as Bylaws - governing the daily operations and strategic decision making in the business -many of the same provisions need to be included. These ar things like the purpose of the entity, the way meetings are called, anc many of the special provisions we discussed in the Bylaw section.

The difference between Bylaws and an Operating Agreement comes down to the nature of the entity and legal definitions on ownership. Meaning the most important sections in an Operating Agreement outline what each Member's unit is, how more Members can be added, and how Members leave or are removed. All of these are important to agree on early in the process, because it is easier to talk about a potential downside at some point in the future versus an immediate problem.

the Members are involved in daily operations, then there may need to be certain restrictions - keep in mind the authority of the Members we mentioned earlier. The Members can agree to which powers an individual Member can exercise and the powers that need more than one - if not all - the Members to agree to in order to exercise. These powers are focused on operations, such as starting or fighting a lawsuit, busing and selling real estate, and more.

Similarly, if a Manager is appointed, the Manager is delegated all or specific powers by the Operating Agreement. This may mean there may be powers and rights reserved for the Members to exercise, that the Manager cannot use. In addition, there may be certain rights the Manager must get the consent of the Members prior to exercising. For example, if the LLC owns a piece of real estate, the standard rule would be the Manager could sell the real estate at any time. However if the Members are not comfortable with such authority being delegated, they can impose limits - either requiring approval of the Member to sell real estate or having such authority remain with the Members.

Voting of the Members is also outlined in the Operating Agreement. Remember, ownership in an LLC is a Membership Unit. However, no two Membership Units have to be the same. Thus, voting can be based upon:

- Owning a Membership Unit

- Percent ownership, or

- As otherwise agreed by the Members.

Remember, an Operating Agreement is a contract between the Member(s) of the LLC. Each State has some laws that cannot be modified, but essentially everything else is based upon what the Members think is best for the business. You can be creative in if and how roles, authority, voting, and more are addressed.

In fact, because this is an agreement between the Member(s), it can be enforced when the only Member signs. The purpose of the Operating Agreement is to give an acceptable structure for the business, as determined by the Members.

Because of this flexibility, an Operating Agreement can be a handful of lines agreed to by the Members. Alternatively, an Operating Agreement can be a behemoth of a document delving into significant detail on any and every part of running a business. Generally something in the middle is appropriate for most businesses.

Article 5: Buy-Sell Agreements

To close out this Handbook, we are going to discuss the Buy-Sell Agreement. A buy-sell lays out how the owners want to sell their ownership interests to another person - with person being the broadest interpretation including other entities.

The core idea behind a buy-sell is the risk that at least one owner will not be able to participate in the business for some reason at some point in the future. We will touch on several of those reasons in this Article. In essence, the buy-sell is an insurance plan: when the unexpected and undesired happens, is the business protected?

A good way to think about it is the buy-sell is an emergency exit. This can range from the collapse of amicability among ownership to death or disability.

Section A: What does a Buy-Sell insure against?

Buy-sell's are effective for a number of situations, which we will discuss briefly.

Sudden death is a tragic and undesired outcome. After all, you are losing a business partner, a friend, or maybe even a spouse. The least important thing upon death is the immediate distribution of assets of the dearly departed. However, that is the purpose of a buy-sell and depending on State, avoidance of probate can be a big motivator.

A properly funded and written buy-sell can remove a significant worry from a widow(er). They don't have to immediately overcome their grief to participate in a business they may want no part of and may even blame. A buy-sell may provide some cold financial comfort and a limited sense of relief that the specifics are already addressed and don't need to be created in a time of emotional turmoil.

Another bad situation covered by a Buy-Sell would be divorce. This comes in two different situations:

1. A married couple started the business and now are divorcing, and

2. One spouse started a business with friends and is going through a divorce.

If the owners are married and divorcing, the question becomes: who owns the business?

Divorces can lead to destructive behavior, regardless of potential consequences. A buy-sell created early can mean the business is addressed specifically and there are tools to work through. Getting something controversial, like a business, off the table may make the divorce process a tiny bit smoother.

If one business owner is getting a divorce, the situation is different. A big tenant of business law is that you get to choose who you want to be in business with. If the divorce goes just right (or wrong) enough, your friend's ex-spouse may be your new business partner, potentially in addition to your friend. It can be easier on the business and on the divorce process itself for the business ownership to be sold. Such a sale means the divorce no longer will directly impact the business. In addition, it means the personal property being contested in the divorce is money instead of the business.

However, you should be cautious in this term. Under certain circumstances, the sale may be fraudulent and undone by the divorce. While there needs to be a plan and an effective sale, there also needs to be the understanding that a certain point, such a sale may be a bad idea and that the appropriate sale would occur after the divorce is finalized.

In the case of personal bankruptcy, the bankruptcy court is going to try and find anyway to pay back creditors of an individual. This includes the power to seize personal property, including ownership in business. If a Judge become involved in the business to pay back the owner's personal debts, the business may find itself in a difficult situation.

Being able to buy out an owner in personal bankruptcy means the court has money to use to settle debts. In addition, the business is much less likely to have a third-party coming in and changing things in order to settle such debts.

A lot of companies are started by friends, but business has a way of being a bigger challenge than expected. This can severely or even permanently hurt those friendships. If the owners get to the point where they cannot stand each other, that situation has to be addressed. This can be someone leaving voluntarily and taking the losses as a part of doing business. Or a buy-sell can "help" someone out the door. If no buy-sell exists, and the situation gets bad enough, friends end up in court - which is likely to be miserable for all involved.

A buy-sell is a contract, which means it can be designed in a manner appropriate for the business and the owners. If multiple are needed, for comfort or for clarity, multiple can be written. If the owners want something simple and straight forward, it can be one buy-sell triggering on various situations. The goal is to cut issues off early and, to the extent possible, avoid lawsuits.

This is an important document regardless of how it is set up for two big reasons.

1. It limits the opportunity for litigation between the owners that can destroy the business. Remember, lawsuits tend to last for at least two years and cost significant amounts of money.

2. A buy-sell is the explicit statement of choice in who to be in business with. Just because you like your co-owner initially, doesn't necessarily mean you like co-owner's spouse or successor.

The goal of the Buy-Sell is to limit some bad situations by putting safeguards in place for the future. At the end of the day, the main function is to plan for bad situations to avoid making those situations worse.

Article 6: Formation Checklist

The best advice I can offer in this Handbook is to talk to a

professional. Attorneys and accountants can be great resources.

Another good resource is your local Small Business Development

Center - find yours at https://www.sba.gov/tools/local-assistance/

sbdc.

The SBDC is a high quality resource with local experts, classes,

mentorship, and more. Most importantly it's a free to you - because it

s funded through the Small Business Administration. Some classes

may require a small fee, but for the most part there is a lot of

expertise for very little price.

included the checklist below as a guideline of everything you are

kely to need when forming an entity.

☐ Decide what business you are going to operate:

　　☐ Write a Business Plan!

　　☐ What is being sold and where (in person, online)?

- ☐ Write a Financial Pro Forma.

- ☐ Write Goals.

- ☐ Decide Ownership - single operator or more?

☐ Pick a Name:

- ☐ Search that name online.

- ☐ Search that name at http://tess2.uspto.gov/bin/gate.exe?

  f=tess&state=4810:hoyqla.1.1 (United States Patent and

  Trademark Office Trademark Search).

- ☐ Search that name at your Secretary of State.

☐ Choose an Entity

- ☐ Make sure it aligns with the Business Plan and your Goals.

☐ File the Registrations

- ☐ With the Secretary of State.

- ☐ With the IRS.

- ☐ With other Taxing entities.

☐ File any applicable licenses

- ☐ Write your Governing Documents:

    - ☐ Operating Agreement or Bylaws

    - ☐ Buy - Sell Agreements?

- ☐ Money Steps:

    - ☐ Obtain Insurance - talk with an Insurance Agent.

        - ☐ Workers Compensation

        - ☐ General Liability

        - ☐ And more.

    - ☐ Get a bookkeeper to make tax season easier.

    - ☐ Hire an accountant.

    - ☐ Get a bank account.

- ☐ Other Steps:

    - ☐ Get your contracts in order!

        - ☐ Service Agreements? Sale of Goods?

        - ☐ Employment Agreements? Independent Contractor

        Agreements?

- ☐ Website Terms of Use?

- ☐ Other?

☐ Protect your Intellectual Property!

- ☐ Patents?

- ☐ Trademarks?

- ☐ Copyrights?

- ☐ Register that Intellectual Property!

- ☐ Trade Secrets? (Don't register but get policies in

  place to protect)

- ☐ Non-Disclosure Agreements?

☐ Employees need guidance.

- ☐ Employee Handbook covering sexual harassment,

  client interactions, social media policies, and

  anything else.

- ☐ Payroll, hire someone to do the withholding!

☐ Insurance - health care, worker's comp, and

everything else.

About the Author

Brian Hanning is the founder and sole attorney for Hanning Law Ltd. He earned a bachelors degree from Colorado State University's College of Business and a juris doctor degree from Michigan State University College of Law. Combining these interests and skill sets sent him on the path towards owning his own firm to connect with and support clients in a more personal and impactful way. Brian is a member of the Colorado Bar and assists entrepreneurs, small businesses, and creative industry clients primarily in the Northern Colorado area.

Brian practices transactional law with a focus on helping small business owners understand what laws can apply to their businesses, and the risks and benefits associated with certain decisions. He also volunteers with Colorado Attorneys for the Arts to share his expertise and hands on client experience with artists around the State.

Outside of work, Brian spends a lot of time with family -most importantly the three family dogs. He enjoys living and working in Fort Collins, Colorado is the abundance of delicious and interesting local coffee shops and microbreweries. Brian ends up at both establishments frequently, perhaps more frequently than his waistline prefers.

CPSIA information can be obtained
at www.ICGtesting.com
Printed in the USA
LVHW010055191119
637666LV00014B/6915

9 781704 318585